The Tutor's Handbook
MATH
Grade 3

Written by Carol Wright

Illustrated by Marilee Harrald-Pilz

Editor: Kathleen Hex
Book Design: Rita Hudson
Cover Design: Riley Wilkinson
Graphic Artist: Randy Shinsato
Cover Photos: Anthony Nex Photography

FS122131 The Tutor's Handbook: Math Grade 3
All rights reserved—Printed in the U.S.A.
23740 Hawthorne Blvd., Torrance, CA 90505

TABLE OF CONTENTS

As a tutor for a young child, consider your role as that of a coach. Picture the coaches you have seen running along the sidelines at local soccer games. They believe in their teams. They encourage, support, advise, and challenge to help the teams achieve victory. As a tutor, you will assume a similar role as you help the child achieve success in third grade math activities.

Patience

Probably one of the most important qualities in a coach or tutor is patience. You have a clear understanding of the math concepts you will be helping the child develop. However, the student will not master these skills overnight. Allow the child sufficient time to explore and practice each skill you present.

Enthusiasm

Just like an athletic coach, the tutor must convey to the student a belief in his or her ability to master the skills. Be an encourager! Call attention to the progress that the child is making in math. Your sincere praise will help the child feel comfortable taking risks and may help him or her develop confidence with math activities.

Process

Soccer coaches are obviously focused on helping their teams win. If you look closely, you will notice that coaches actually spend much of the time helping the players learn the process of winning a game. As you help the student develop a variety of math strategies, try to focus a significant amount of energy on the things the child is doing to solve the problems. Encourage the student to talk out loud as he or she thinks about and works on a problem. Pose thoughtful questions about the process used to solve a problem. This is more helpful than simply marking answers right or wrong.

Make it a common practice to ask the child to tell you how he or she got the answer to a problem. If you discover the child began solving an addition problem in the tens place, ask the child why he or she began that way. Just as the athletic coach does not allow the team to practice over and over the wrong way to play, help the student succeed by talking about the process that will help him or her reach the correct answer. Resist the temptation to just tell your student the correct answer as this will result in little long term learning. Pose questions about the problem that will challenge the child to explore and utilize the different strategies he or she is developing. When the child correctly solves a problem, encourage him or her to describe the process used to solve it.

In your important role of tutor as coach, have patience with your student! Remember that the child is learning as fast as he or she can. Be enthusiastic about learning! Your excitement and encouragement may help the child improve his or her attitude toward math. Finally, focus on the process of learning! It is just as important as getting the right answer.

GRADE LEVEL EXPECTATIONS

In third grade, students apply the skills mastered in the earlier elementary grades to solve more difficult and sophisticated math problems. These standards for instruction are set by the National Council of Teachers of Mathematics.

Numbers and Computation

Third graders should be able to

- understand and practice place value up to 100,000

- add and subtract up to 4 digits with and without regrouping (borrowing and carrying)

- round numbers to the nearest ten, hundred, and thousand

- estimate, approximate, and use mental math

- work with money by adding, subtracting, and counting change

- memorize multiplication facts through 9

- use inverse operations to check work (addition to check subtraction, division to check multiplication)

- understand the special properties of 0 and 1 in multiplication and division (multiplying by 0 equals 0, a number multiplied by 1 equals itself)

- identify and compare fractions

- read mixed numbers (for example 3½)

Geometry

Third graders should be able to

- explore both two- and three-dimensional shapes

- use appropriate vocabulary to describe figures

- identify lines, line segments, rays, and right angles

- recognize and identify sphere, cube, prism, rectangular prism, cone, and cylinder

- recognize congruent shapes (shapes that are the same shape and size)

- identify lines of symmetry

- find the area and perimeter of common figures

Patterns

Third graders should be able to

- identify, create, and extend geometric and number patterns

- use the 1–100 number and multiplication charts

- skip count by 2, 3, 4, 5, and 10

GRADE LEVEL EXPECTATIONS

Data Analysis, Statistics, and Probability

Third graders should be able to

- collect, organize, graph, and interpret data

- use tally marks to organize data

- use and create line graphs, bar graphs, pictographs, and tables

- determine the probability (likelihood) of an event happening

Measurement

Third graders should be able to

- use U.S. customary and metric units to measure length, liquid volume, weight or mass

- estimate and accurately measure common objects

- tell time to the minute

- find elapsed time

- use and find information on a calendar

Problem Solving

Third graders should be able to

- develop a variety of problem-solving strategies

- use previous activities to plan strategies

- analyze problems to determine the necessary information and the unnecessary information

- recognize patterns that may help solve the problem

- sequence or prioritize the information given

- recognize the appropriate time to use a particular strategy

- describe how the problem and the strategy used are related

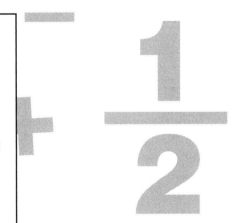

Assess Skills

As you begin working with the child, determine his or her strengths and weaknesses in a given area. Give the child the pretest provided for each section. His or her performance on the pretest will help you determine appropriate areas for skill development. Try to determine the child's level of competence in a particular area by asking questions. What word might be used to show subtraction? How do we show multiplication?

Helpful Hint: Collect all necessary materials before the session begins. Children will lose interest if the tutor has to search for supplies.

Review Concepts

Begin each session by discussing concepts covered in the previous session. Pose questions that encourage the child to show his or her understanding. What did we cover in last week's session? When you are comparing large numbers, which place value should you look at first? Why? Provide clarification and work specific problems together as needed.

If the child has completed assignments since the previous session, review the work together. Avoid the temptation to merely mark all of the problems right or wrong. Talk with the student about how the work was completed and review information as needed. Working from a wrong answer to the correct answer frequently results in a more thorough understanding of the math concept. Consider asking, "What made you think that?" or "How did you get that answer?" for correct answers as well as for wrong answers. The student gets in the habit of scrutinizing answers and reflecting on his or her thinking.

Introduce New Concepts

After reviewing, introduce the new concepts to be covered during the session. Whenever possible, provide concrete objects such as beans, toothpicks, cotton balls, or other available objects for the child to use while working. These hands-on experiences help the child fully understand the concept and prepares him or her for exploring abstract mathematical principles. Encourage the child to talk out loud while working out problems. Listening to the child's thought process will help you assess his or her understanding of the concept.

Use the correct vocabulary as you help the child learn new concepts. If you are working with inequality signs, call them "less than" and "greater than." Some shortcuts may be helpful such as the arrow points to the smaller number in inequality problems. These strategies, however, must not replace learning the important mathematical vocabulary. In later grades, using and appropriately applying a strong mathematical vocabulary is very important.

Practice Makes Perfect

Practice is a very important component of any tutoring session. Provide a few problems for the child to practice during the session, but be careful that the practice is not mindless and repetitive. This book provides a number of practice pages, but they are in no way exhaustive. Use them as a guide to help you create additional problems to ensure that the student thoroughly understands the concepts.

Helpful Hint:
Watch the child as he or she completes the practice items, being alert for any clarification that may be needed.

Give careful thought to the practice you provide. Make sure the practice will require the student to think and apply the concepts he or she is working on. Once the child has demonstrated mastery, be careful not to assume he or she knows the skill. Instead, provide regular opportunities for the child to review prior concepts and practice current ones in a thoughtful, meaningful manner.

Ending the Session

If appropriate, give the child an assignment to complete independently before the next session. It is often helpful to have the child explain how he or she will complete the assigned problems before ending the session. The practice you provide will not extend and challenge the child's mathematical understanding if he or she is unsure how to proceed or practices a concept incorrectly.

Before ending the session, make sure the child has the necessary tools to complete the work. Pencils, paper, multiplication chart, 1–100 number chart, and a box of counting beans will help ensure success on the assignment. Finally, review the session with the child. Have him or her explain to you the concepts learned and the process or strategies used during the session. End the session on a positive and encouraging note. Remember to answer any questions the student may have before sending him or her off.

Play Games

Playing games together is a wonderful way to practice and review concepts! Rolling dice, totaling the value of a hand of cards, or using play money are fun ways to reinforce many math concepts. Make a game board from sturdy cardboard. Use tokens or checkers as game pieces. Encourage the child to create his or her own game using addition, subtraction, or multiplication. Talking about the things you are thinking as you play the game models an important strategy for your child.

Use Modeling

Helpful Hint: Pose open-ended, thought-provoking questions to the student as you help him or her work out math problems.

It will be helpful to the student if you model some of the strategies that you want to see him or her develop. As you are working through problems together, suggest making a list to organize the data. Would it help to make a chart? Show the child how to draw a picture or make a model that will help him or her solve the problem. Encourage the child to look for and articulate patterns in the problems he or she is working to solve. Suggesting, modeling, and trying out a variety of strategies together will help the child develop confidence with these strategies and will increase the likelihood of applying these strategies in the future.

Explore Math Facts

Third graders need to begin memorizing the answers to addition, subtraction, multiplication, and division problems. Flash cards are one possible way to practice basic math facts. To make memorization more exciting, roll two dice and ask the student to add, subtract, multiply, or divide the numbers. When the child becomes comfortable with this, vary the difficulty by using three or four dice. The dots on the sides provide useful support

to beginning students. A deck of cards or dominos can be used for more fun practice.

Helpful Hint: Use a table cloth or place mats to reduce noise levels when working with math manipulatives such as blocks, counting squares, dominos, or dice.

Beat the Clock

Many children love to compete against themselves and others. When helping the child learn math facts, record the time it takes him or her to get through the set of flashcards. Review the same cards during following sessions, timing each. Compare the times and ask what the child notices about them. Graphing the time results might motivate the child to beat his or her time. For optimal success, keep the number of flash cards reasonable for the child. If adding the time factor becomes stressful for the student, it may be a sign that he or she needs to review his or her understanding of the concept. Keep this practice fun, not overwhelming!

Vary Activities

Keep the child's attention span in mind as you plan the session. Vary the activities to ensure that the student is working with paper and pencil, doing math in his head, using tangible objects, and talking about his or her strategies. If he or she is working on developing measurement skills, consider having the child get up and actually measure items in the room. Varying both the length and the type of activities will ensure that the student gets the most from the session.

Read a Book

For some of your sessions together, consider using a favorite children's book as a springboard to help explore a mathematical concept from a different perspective. (Refer to the Literature List on pages 61 and 62.) Read the book and discuss the math presented. Write any math problems from the book on a sheet of paper and solve them together. Did you get the same answer as the character in the book? Can you think of other problems you can try to solve?

Use a Newspaper

A newspaper is another useful tool to reinforce concepts while providing a tangible reminder that math is used in everyday life. Provide a list of numbers for the child to find in the newspaper such as a street address, the date of the paper, a number that names a distance, or the score in a game. The

student can also cut out random numbers and organize them in a particular way, for example, from largest to smallest. Ask the student to round the numbers to the nearest ten, hundred, or thousand. Cut out graphs or tables and discuss them with the student. The possibilities are limitless!

Student Survey

The student survey is designed to help you determine how the student feels about math. Before beginning the tutoring sessions, use the survey to facilitate a discussion about the child's math abilities. At the conclusion of the tutoring sessions, use the survey to assess how well the child has progressed. Ask the child to answer the questions on the survey to the best of his or her ability, but keep it as stress-free as possible.

After the survey is complete, it is important to discuss the answers with the child. Often, other questions will arise during the discussion. Does it help when you draw a picture to solve the problem? Do you find it easy or difficult to use a ruler? What was

> **Helpful Hint:** Use this discussion time to find out about the child's interests. Using these interests during instruction and practice will help motivate and keep the child interested.

the most important thing you learned during tutoring? What else would you like to learn about math?

 # Student Survey

Circle your answer for each question.

1 How much do you enjoy learning math?

a little   some   a lot

2 How good are you at math?

not very good   okay   very good

3 How good are you at helping other kids do math?

not very good   okay   very good

4 Would you like to spend more time doing math?

no   maybe   yes

Finish each sentence.

5 The part of math I like best is _____

_____

6 The part of math I like least is _____

_____

As you work with children to help them deepen their math skills it is important that you help them recognize that they are working to develop skills which they will find useful and necessary in life. Children have probably seen adults who find it difficult to figure out the tip after enjoying a meal in a restaurant. They may have seen cashiers who are unsure of how to make change in a store. Part of the tutoring sessions should, therefore, focus on helping children see that math is all around them.

Children often receive the message that math is memorizing many facts. This is one aspect of math which makes completing math problems easier. It is important to help them see that measuring, patterns, geometry, determining how likely something is to happen, and explaining a reason for something is also math. Figuring out if he or she has enough money to buy a new video game, the batting average of a favorite baseball star, or how long before a movie begins are all experiences that help children value math skills.

Language Arts

Children have worked hard to become confident readers and enjoy using this skill. A number of excellent children's books have been published which serve as terrific discussion starters with third graders. Start by reading *The King's Chessboard* by David Birch (Dial, 1988). It is a story of a wise man who requests that his reward begin with a single grain of rice. The reward is doubled for each square of the chessboard. Extend this idea to the child's life. If the child earned an allowance of one

cent the first week and it was doubled each week, how long would it take to save enough to treat the family to lunch at a fast food restaurant?

Third graders may enjoy examining the words and letters in books from a mathematical perspective. Write the 26 letters of the alphabet vertically on a piece of blank paper. Choose a page in a favorite book, an article in a newspaper, or a page in a children's magazine and use tallies to record the number of times each letter appears on that page. Repeat this with a book in another language and compare the results. Create a chart or graph the results. Does the type of book used matter? After reviewing the results, repeat the activity but look at the length of words in the selection. How many two letter words are used? Three letters? More than eight letters?

Art

Children who enjoy art are likely to become more engaged in practicing their math skills when they are encouraged to create a work of art using differ-  ent geometric shapes. Tesselations are repeated geometric figures or patterns that fill a space completely without any gaps. Once they have been introduced to tessalations, challenge children to discover them in wrapping paper, tile flooring, different fabrics, and brick walkways. They will be able to examine quilts and talk about the patterns they see in a variety of them. After exploration, children can try using lines and shapes to design their own quilt squares or other works of art.

Science

Math and science have many tangible connections. Examining a variety of creatures is a natural springboard for a wide assortment of mathematical questioning. When watching earthworms, children can predict how long they are and then actually measure them. How do astronomers measure the distance between planets? After studying dinosaurs, what things in your world can you find that are about the same length? Children who are working to learn multiplication facts practice them naturally when they create a chart to determine the number of legs on spiders or ants. Students who are studying the human body will enjoy collecting number data for a chart. How many bones? Teeth? Heart chambers? How much blood does the average body contain? Water?

Social Studies

Social studies also has many natural mathematical connections. Collecting data of the opinions of friends is highly motivating as third graders have many natural questions which interest them. They may pose questions about the favorite food served in the cafeteria or at a popular restaurant. Children can create a graph to show the amount of food eaten versus food thrown away. Examining and drawing conclusions from data helps make math skills meaningful to children. Topics might include the amounts of time children watch television or the number of commercials in prime time aimed at young children.

Math All Around Us

Use real-world experiences to develop math skills. How much should the child's favorite fast food meal cost based on studying the menu? Is the combo meal really a better buy? Which size drink or popcorn is the best buy? What shapes do you notice in the designs of buildings in the neighborhood? How much change should you get back at the toy store? How many miles is it to the nearest amusement park? Is an annual pass at your favorite amusement park a good purchase? How many times would you need to use it to make it worthwhile? Use brochures and advertisements to create real-life math problems.

> **Helpful Hints:**
> Varying the kinds of activities you do with the student will help maintain interest and enthusiasm.

Examine an ad from a local grocery store. If you only bought items on sale, what meals could you prepare for your family? Calculating the cost of multiple items provides practice with multiplication. Determining the value of double coupons enables the child to practice multiplying by two.

CONCEPTS THIRD GRADERS SHOULD KNOW

- place value to 100,000
- addition and subtraction to 4 digits
- rounding to the nearest ten, hundred and thousand
- estimation
- addition and subtraction of money amounts
- multiplication facts through 9
- inverse operations to check work
- the special properties of 0 and 1
- fractions
- mixed numbers

What's the Value?

Make a place value chart by turning a piece of paper horizontally, dividing it in thirds, and writing the labels *hundreds, tens,* and *ones* at the top of each section. Write the digits 0 through 9 on blank index cards. Make more than one set so the child can practice naming the same digit in more than one column. Select three cards and place one in each section on the place value chart and ask the child to read the number. On scratch paper, practice writing the number in expanded form to help the child understand the value of the number they have read. (873 = 800 + 70 + 3.) As the child becomes proficient with three places, add a column for thousands and then ten thousands. The same skill may be practiced using dice, a deck of cards, or a numbered spinner from any game.

Helpful Hint: Remind the child that a comma is used between the thousands and hundreds place to help read larger numbers.

The Numbers are in the Bag

Write the numbers 0 through 9 on 2" x 2" cards. Place the number cards in a bag. Each player makes three short lines on some scratch paper. Players take turns drawing a number from the bag and writing it on one of the three lines. Continue until all players have filled all of their lines. Who has the biggest number? The smallest? What is the strategy for making the largest number? What would you do to make the smallest number? Extend to include more place values as the child becomes more proficient with the concept. Vary this activity by having the players arrange the numbers in ascending or descending order. What number is in the hundreds place? The tens place? The ones place? Ask the players to add all of the numbers. Subtract the smallest number from the largest.

Numbers in Print

Provide a variety of newspapers or magazines. Have the child find two-, three-, and four-digit numbers, depending on the comfort level he or she has built with place value. Invite the child to cut out the numbers and glue them on another piece of paper. Review place value by posing questions based on the numbers the child has cut out. Which number has a 4 in the hundreds place? A 6 in the tens place?

Rounding Around the World

Help the child consult an almanac or encyclopedia for population counts in various cities or states. Ask the child to round several numbers. Which city has the highest population? The lowest? Approximately how many people live in your city or state? Round to the nearest thousand.

Helpful hint: Remind the student when to round up (five or more) and when to round down (four or less). The same rule applies for rounding to the nearest hundred or thousand.

Making Comparisons

Research the length of several dinosaurs. Which dinosaur was the longest? The shortest?

Remind the child that when comparing two numbers, he or she should always start with the digit in the highest place value (at the left). If the digits are the same, move to the next digit (to the right) and compare them the same way. With practice, this skill becomes second nature for children and helps prepare them for working with larger numbers.

All in Order

Use an almanac to locate the height of several famous buildings in your state. Analyze the information and arrange the buildings from tallest to shortest. Find the cost of four favorite cars for the year. Which is the cheapest? Most expensive? Arrange the costs in order from least to most expensive. What is the difference between the least and most expensive?

Money

Have the child reach into a change jar and grab a handful of coins. The child should be able to name and write the total value of the coins. Encourage the child to create addition and subtraction problems to practice.

Helpful Hint: Remind the child of the importance of including the dollar sign and decimal point in money problems.

Use this technique to practice counting change. Remind the child that he or she can count change by creating and solving a subtraction problem or counting forward from the amount spent to the amount given.

Shopping Spree

Cut out items with prices from a catalog and glue them on cards or small pieces of paper. Ask the child to shop for three items. What is the total cost of these items? How much change should you get from a twenty dollar bill?

Valuable Names

Create a chart listing the letters of the alphabet from A to Z. Assign a value to each letter: A = \$.01, B = \$.02, and so on. How much is your name worth? Determine the values of other names and compare the values. Encourage the child to think aloud while working. Why are different names different values?

Practicing Computation

Most third graders are familiar with adding and subtracting numbers with and without regrouping or carrying. They are also learning multiplication and division facts through 9. They should be exposed to reading and solving number problems which are written both horizontally and vertically. If the child has difficulty correctly solving problems which are written horizontally, encourage him or her to rewrite the problem vertically. As this skill becomes more developed, the format of the problem should not matter as the child is better able to visualize the problem.

Challenge the student to create and solve as many computation problems as possible using his or her surroundings. If there are three desks in each row and there are five rows, how many desks are in the classroom? If the child has ten blue marbles and eleven purple marbles, how many marbles does he or she have in all? Point out that using inverse operations is an easy way to check answers. Show the child how to use addition to check subtraction or division to check multiplication and vice versa.

A Sea of Numbers

Write each number in expanded form.

1 4,682

2 796

_____

_____

Write each number in standard form.

3 6,000 + 80 + 2 = _____

4 3,000 + 400 + 60 + 9 _____

Put the numbers in order from greatest to least.

5 298, 372, 621 _____

6 571, 592, 538 _____

Round to the nearest ten.

7 429 _____

8 381 _____

Round to the nearest hundred.

9 792 _____

10 3, 684 _____

Write the money amount.

11 1 quarter, 2 dimes, 3 nickels, 2 pennies _____

Add or subtract.

12
```
  86
+ 23
```

13
```
$5.72
+  1.79
```

14
```
  228
  307
+  62
```

15
```
  67
- 32
```

16
```
$8.73
- 4.89
```

17
```
 8,472
-3,761
```

16
reproducible

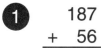

A Whale of Math Fun

Add. Check your work using subtraction.

1 187
  + 56

2 152
  + 76

3 24
  + 78

4 $1.62
  + 2.03

5 76 + 12 + 83 = _____

6 38 + _____ = 92

Add across and down to complete each box.

7

+	62	42	
	38	37	

8

+	52	8	
	37	72	

Round each number to the nearest ten and the nearest hundred.

9 1,308 _____ _____
            hundred   ten

10 8,676 _____ _____
            hundred   ten

Give the value for each underlined number.

11 8,3<u>6</u>4 _____

12 <u>3</u>,187 _____

FS122131 The Tutor's Handbook: Math Grade 3

Name

Seahorse Subtraction

Subtract. Use addition to check your work.

1
72
− 38

2
722
− 581

3
862
− 439

4
$6.05
− $4.76

5 3,814 − 2,489 = _____

6 811 − _____ = 275

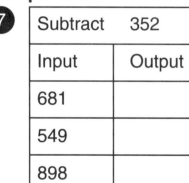

Complete each chart.

7

Subtract	352
Input	Output
681	
549	
898	

8

Subtract	175
Input	Output
875	
980	
374	

Write the numbers from greatest to least.

9 3,212   3,867   3,107   _____

10 587   215   403   _____

Subtract the smallest number from the largest number.

11 4,881   3,611   1,768   _____

FS122131 The Tutor's Handbook: Math Grade 3

 **Name** _____

Super Sea Stars

Solve each problem. Watch the signs carefully.

1
```
   672
 −  84
```

2
```
  3,211
+ 1,789
```

3
```
   $7.87
 +  2.38
```

4
```
  4,521
− 1,812
```

5 _____ + 868 = 6,877

6 877 − _____ = 329

Add across and down to complete the box.

7

+	112	306	
	486	519	

Subtract across and down to complete the box.

8

−	987	412	
	683	233	

Give the value for the underlined number.

9 3,8<u>2</u>7 _____

10 <u>6</u>,209 _____

11 5,8<u>8</u>1 _____

 Name

Swimming with Numbers

Write each number in expanded form.

1 8,274

_____

2 478

_____

Write each number in standard form.

3 4,000 + 600 + 20 + 7 = _____

4 200 + 40 + 2 = _____

Put the numbers in order from least to greatest.

5 2,472   3,612   3,678 _____

Round each to the nearest ten.

6 728 _____

7 694 _____

Round each to the nearest hundred.

8 1,862 _____

9 488 _____

Write the amount.

10 1 quarter, 3 dimes, 4 nickels, 4 pennies _____

Solve each problem.

11
```
   702
   439
 + 312
```

12
```
   589
 - 213
```

13 811 + 674 = _____

14 $1.73 + $2.38 = _____

FS122131 The Tutor's Handbook: Math Grade 3

CONCEPTS THIRD GRADERS SHOULD KNOW

- geometric and number patterns
- 1–100 number chart
- multiplication chart
- skip count by 2, 3, 4, 5, and 10

The 1–100 Number Chart

Introduce the 1–100 number chart (page 23) by asking the child to look for neighbors on the chart whose sum is 13 (6 and 7) and whose sum is 7 (3 and 4). Use the chart to solve other simple addition and subtraction problems. Looking for patterns will help the student identify shortcuts to help solve more difficult problems.

The 1–100 number chart can also be used to practice place value. Cover all of the numbers with a 1 in the ones place. What pattern do you see? Cover all the numbers with a 5 in the tens place. What pattern do you see? Cover all the numbers whose digits equal 8 when added. What is the pattern?

Skip Counting

Skip counting means skipping numbers as you count by groups other than one. To skip count by 3, place a counter on the number 3 on the 1–100 number chart. Skip 2 squares and place another counter on the third number. Continue covering numbers for 3 rows. Ask the child to name the numbers and describe the pattern. Repeat the

process with other numbers. As children become more comfortable, vary the difficulty of the patterns you present. Start at 36. Skip count by 3 and end at 52. Which numbers will you cover? Name the odd numbers between 63 and 87. Ask the child to practice skip counting as he or she jumps rope, saying one number with each jump.

Sequencing

Help the child identify a sequence pattern on the 1–100 number chart (24, 27, ___, 33, 36, ___). Have him or her cover each number given in the sequence with a counting bean. Encourage the child to look for a pattern to help name the missing numbers. Practice both forward and backward number sequences to help the child develop this skill. Remind him or her that it is important to look at the entire list of numbers before looking for the answer. Give the child a list of numbers in a sequence. Would 35 be in this sequence? Why or why not?

Helpful Hint: Using counters (dried beans or popcorn seeds) to cover the numbers on the 1-100 number chart enables the child to look for patterns and use the chart again and again.

15...20...
25...30...
35...

Multiplication Table

Recognizing patterns helps children grasp and apply multiplication facts quickly. When skip counting has been practiced on the 1–100 number chart, the child is ready to begin using the multiplication table. The child should be able to explain that multiplication is repeated addition. It is different from addition because only equal groups of objects are added. The multiplication problem 3 x 4 is the same as the addition problem 4 + 4 + 4. Recognizing the patterns and memorizing the multiplication facts will enable the child to solve problems quickly.

Check the student's math book for a multiplication table or create one together. Challenge the child to explore the table and look for patterns in the same way he or she uses the 1–100 number chart. What pattern do you see across the 2 row or down the 2 column? Which row on the chart would you get if you doubled the 3 row? If you add the 3 row to the 4 row, which row on the chart will you get? What pattern do you see in the 9 row?

Charts

Helping the student organize information in a chart often helps him or her see the pattern more readily and enables him or her to solve problems more quickly. Create a chart for the number of days in a week. The rows give the number of weeks and the columns give the number of days in that many weeks. Under 1 would be 7, under 2 would be 14. Challenge the child to extend the chart. Ask him or her to create new charts to organize the number of wheels on tricycles or cars.

Fact Families

Fact families are addition and subtraction or multiplication and division facts that use the same numbers. There are usually four facts in each family. Write out a math problem that the child knows, such as 7 + 8 = 15. Help the child see that he or she also knows that 8 + 7 = 15, 15 − 8 = 7 and 15 − 7 = 8. Give the child the numbers in a fact family and ask him or her to write all of the problems. Try using both addition/subtraction and multiplication/division. Practice with fact families helps the child memorize basic math facts.

 Name _____

1–100 Number Chart

Use counting beans to cover number patterns on the chart. Use it to help you find the next number in a sequence of numbers.

1	2	3	4	5	6	7	8	9	10
11	12	13	14	15	16	17	18	19	20
21	22	23	24	25	26	27	28	29	30
31	32	33	34	35	36	37	38	39	40
41	42	43	44	45	46	47	48	49	50
51	52	53	54	55	56	57	58	59	60
61	62	63	64	65	66	67	68	69	70
71	72	73	74	75	76	77	78	79	80
81	82	83	84	85	86	87	88	89	90
91	92	93	94	95	96	97	98	99	100

Note to tutor: Create number patterns for the student to find. Practice using the number chart to complete addition, subtraction, or simple multiplication problems.

FS122131 The Tutor's Handbook: Math Grade 3

 **Name**

Perfect Patterns

Complete each number pattern.

1 0, 8, 15, 21, 26, _____, _____, _____.

2 33, 36, 39, 42, _____, _____, _____.

3 Jenny uses 4 buttons for each puppet she makes. Complete the chart.

puppets	1	2	3	4	5
buttons	4				

Fill in the correct numbers for each section of the outer circle.

4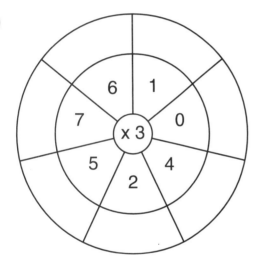

5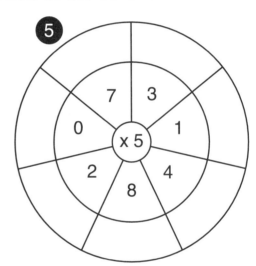

Write four number sentences for each fact family.

6 7 8 15

_____

_____

_____

_____

7 3 7 21

_____

_____

_____

_____

8 4 8 32

_____

_____

_____

_____

FS122131 The Tutor's Handbook: Math Grade 3

Math Blooms

Multiply.

1   3
    x 2

2   8
    x 3

3   6
    x 2

4 $9 \times 5 =$ _____

5 $4 \times 4 =$ _____

Divide.

6 $7\overline{)63}$

7 $6\overline{)54}$

8 $16 \div 2 =$ _____

9 $40 \div 5 =$ _____

Use the rule to finish each chart.

10

x	3
4	
1	
3	
6	
8	

11

x	2
0	
5	
6	
7	
8	

12

÷	5
10	
25	
40	
35	
15	

Fill in the missing numbers.

13

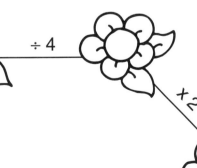

÷ 4

÷ 5

x 3

x 2

÷ 3

40

FS122131 The Tutor's Handbook: Math Grade 3

Name

Growing in Math

Multiply.

1   7
      x 6

2   7
      x 7

3   6
      x 6

4 8 x 4 = _____

5 7 x 9 = _____

Divide. Think of multiplication.

6 3)15

7 6)42

8 48 ÷ 8 = _____

9 45 ÷ 9 = _____

Use the rule to finish each chart.

10

x	7	6	8	5
7				

11

÷	64	56	72	24
8				

Give the 3 other facts in each fact family.

12 6 x 8 = 48

13 56 ÷ 8 = 7

14 42 ÷ 7 = 6

_____

_____

_____

FS122131 The Tutor's Handbook: Math Grade 3

Name _____

Pattern Power

Complete each number pattern.

1 365, 465, _____, _____, _____.

2 1, 8, 15, _____, _____, _____.

Finish the chart.

3

1	2	3	4	5	6
3					

5...
4...
3...
2...
1...

BLASTOFF!!

Fill in the correct numbers for each section of the outer circle.

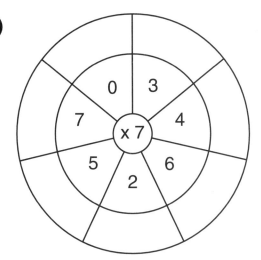

4

0 3
7 × 7 4
5 6
2

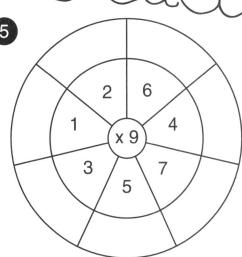

5

2 6
1 × 9 4
3 7
5

Write 4 number sentences for each fact family.

6 7 9 16

_____

_____

_____

_____

7 4 7 28

_____

_____

_____

_____

A *ray* is a part of a line with one endpoint. A *line segment* is a part of a straight line that has two endpoints. It is named by the letters located at the end of the line segment. A *polygon* is a shape that is formed with three or more line segments. The point where two sides meet is called an *angle*. A *right angle* is formed when the line segments make a square corner. Two figures are congruent if they are exactly the same size and shape.

CONCEPTS THIRD GRADERS SHOULD KNOW

- two- and three-dimensional shapes
- angles, line segments, rays, right angles
- congruent shapes and lines of symmetry
- ordered pairs

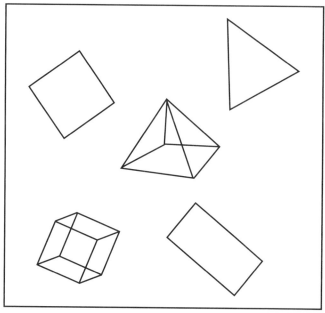

Angles

Make a moveable angle model to help the child practice naming and measuring angles. Cut two 2" x 10" rectangles out of stiff cardboard. Punch a hole in the end of each piece and place a fastener through the holes. Use the device to measure a variety of objects around the room—the corner of a table or the edge of a window. Encourage the child to check other angles and to determine if each one is larger or smaller than a right angle.

Polygons

Have the child draw a polygon with five sides. Count the sides together. Encourage the child to draw another five-sided polygon that looks different from the first one. How many different polygons can you draw with five sides? Try this with a variety of polygons such as hexagon (6 sides), octagon (8 sides), and decagon (10 sides).

Line of Symmetry

Practice looking at a variety of shapes and objects to identify the line of symmetry. A small mirror is a fun way to reinforce this concept. Hold the mirrow perpendicular to the shape and find the image repeated. The place where the mirror is held is the line of symmetry. Find the page in an encyclopedia or dictionary that shows flags from different countries. What shapes are used on the flags? Which ones have a line of symmetry? Which letters in the alphabet are symmetrical? Try this for both capital and lower case letters.

> **Helpful Hint:** When a figure can be folded in half and the two parts match exactly, the figure is symmetric. Figures can have more than one line of symmetry or even no line of symmetry.

Geometric Vocabulary

As you are walking or driving, ask the child to point out objects with right angles. Practice counting the sides and angles of common household objects. As you read a book with the child, have him or her identify shapes encountered. Review important terms by using them to give clues for an object in the room. Ask questions such as: How many objects can you find that are made of rectangles? Can you find a cylinder in the cupboard?

Nets

Carefully take apart different-sized boxes at the seams so that they are flattened, but still in one piece. These flattened figures are called the nets of the boxes. Have the student practice forming different nets into solids. For additional practice, have the child draw different nets on graph paper with large squares. He or she can cut out the net, color it, then fold on the lines to discover the solid form he or she has created.

> **Helpful Hint:**
> **Guess and test is a powerful problem-solving strategy! Encourage the child to talk about why some guesses or tests did not work and why the successful one did!**

Flip, Slide, and Turn

A *flip* is to move a figure over a line so that the figure faces in the opposite direction. A *slide* is to move a figure along a straight line without changing direction. A *turn* is to move a figure along a curved path around a point either clockwise or counterclockwise.

Flips, slides, and turns are physical motions encountered when common objects are moved. Practice each of these concepts by cutting two congruent triangles out of an index card. Place the two triangles on top of each other on the table. Move the top one and ask the child to identify what the move shows: flip, slide, or turn. Try this using various objects to practice flipping, sliding and turning.

Coordinates

Geometry also introduces children to reading coordinates, or pairs of numbers. On graph paper, draw a horizontal line and a vertical line to form four right angles. Add arrows to the ends of both lines. The horizontal line is called the *x-axis* and the vertical line is called the *y-axis*. The point where the x-axis and y-axis cross is zero. Starting at zero, number the points along the x- and y-axis. Then mark the coordinates on the grid and have the student name each coordinate. The first number gives the location on the x-axis and the second number gives the location on the y-axis. Later, provide coordinates and have the student plot the points on the grid.

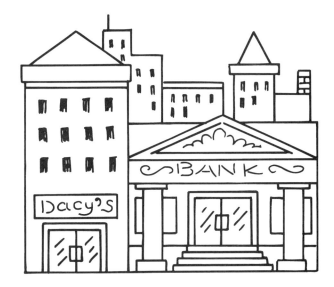

 Name

Galloping Geometrics

**Write the correct name under each space figure.
Then use the figure to complete the chart.**

1

figure	corners	flat edges	flat faces	curved faces
_____				
 _____				

Write *yes* or *no*.

2 Are the figures congruent?

_____

3 Does the dashed line show a line of symmetry?

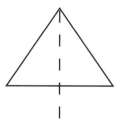

_____

4 Plot the coordinates on the grid. Connect the points. What shape did you make?

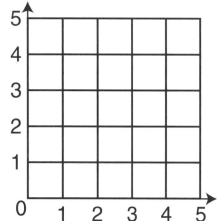

(1, 2) (5, 2) (1, 5) (5, 5)

_____

FS122131 The Tutor's Handbook: Math Grade 3

 **Name** _____

Ready? Set? Go, Geometry!

Look at each clock. Tell if the angle formed by the hands is a right angle, greater than a right angle, or less than a right angle.

_____   _____   _____   _____

Tell how many line segments are in each letter.

5 _____   **6** _____   **7** _____

Draw a line of symmetry through each shape.

 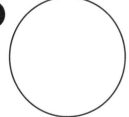   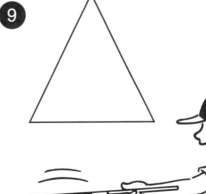

FS122131 The Tutor's Handbook: Math Grade 3

Name

Geometry Goals

Look at each pair. Are they congruent? Write *yes* or *no*.

1 _____ 2 _____ 3 _____

The shaded figure shows how the figure was moved. Write *flip*, *slide*, or *turn* to tell how it was moved.

 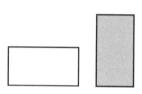 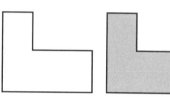

4 _____ 5 _____ 6 _____

7 Plot the coordinates on the grid. Connect the points. What shape did you make?

(3, 1) (6, 8) (10, 1)

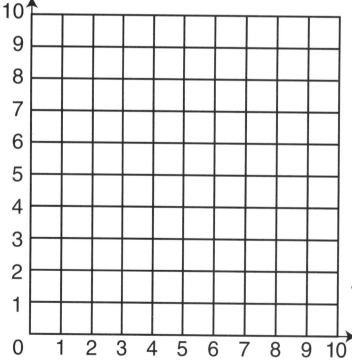

32
reproducible

 **Name**

Gliding Geometry

Name the solid each net forms.

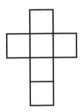 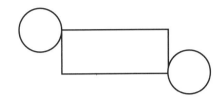 

1 _____ **2** _____ **3** _____

Write the space figure name for each object.

  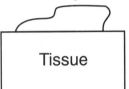

Tissue

4 _____ **5** _____ **6** _____

7 _____ **8** _____

Draw each shape.

9 Triangle **10** Rectangle **11** Hexagon

FS122131 The Tutor's Handbook: Math Grade 3

Geometry Greatness

Write the name of each figure or shape.

_____   _____   _____

Write *yes* or *no*.

Are the two shapes congruent?

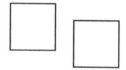

Draw a dashed line through the figure to show the line of symmetry.

 _____   _____

Write the best description for each angle: right angle, greater than a right angle, or less than a right angle.

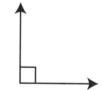

 _____   _____

CONCEPTS THIRD GRADERS SHOULD KNOW

- U.S. customary measurement
- metric measurement
- time to the minute
- elapsed time
- calendar
- area, perimeter, and volume

Length

Ask the child to suggest the appropriate unit to use to measure paintings or drawings. After measuring an item, pose questions to help the child consider the information. If the painting is 1½ feet wide, can I hang it in a space that is 21 inches?

Practice length measurements by playing this game. One player gives a measurement and the other tries to draw a line that equals that length. Switch roles. Use a ruler to verify the actual length of each line. The person whose line is closer to the accurate measurement wins a point. Practice with both U.S. customary and metric units.

Look up a variety of sports records in which the distance is measured in meters (for example, swimming or track). How many feet is that? By how much did the new record beat the previous record? If possible, go outside and actually measure the same distance.

Perimeter

Choose five rectangular objects such as a tissue box, an envelope, a magazine, a picture, and a cereal box. Ask the child to arrange the objects in order from the one with the smallest perimeter to the one with the largest perimeter. Use a ruler to check actual perimeter and compare this information with the original estimate. How much bigger is the perimeter of the largest object than the smallest object?

> **Helpful Hint:**
> Area is the number of square units that will fit inside a region. Perimeter is the distance around the outside of an object or figure.

Area

Draw plane figures of various rectangular objects on graph paper. Help the child determine the area for each object. Which has the greatest area? The smallest? As a challenge, ask the child to compare the area of the object to the perimeter of the same object.

Help the child use appropriate tools to measure a room and the main objects in the room. Transfer this information to graph paper to represent the current arrangement of the furniture. Using this information, is there another way to arrange this room? Practice various arrangements on the graph paper and select a favorite. If possible, test your ideas by using the map to help the child rearrange the room. Try this method using the child's classroom or make a model of his or her favorite ice cream shop.

Metric	U.S. Customary
length 1 centimeter = 10 millimeters 1 decimeter = 10 centimeters 1 meter = 10 decimeters **mass/weight** 1 kilogram = 1,000 grams **capacity** 1 liter = 1,000 milliliters	**length** 1 foot = 12 inches 1 yard = 3 feet 1 mile = 5,280 feet **mass/weight** 1 pound = 16 ounces 1 ton = 2,000 pounds **capacity** 1 cup = 8 fluid ounces 1 pint = 2 cups 1 quart = 2 pints 1 gallon = 4 quarts

Capacity

Look on a food pyramid to determine how many glasses of milk a third grader should drink each day. If a child drinks 4 glasses of milk a day for a week, how many pints would he or she drink? Quarts? Gallons? How many would that child drink in a month? A year?

Encourage the student to suggest appropriate measurement units for various objects. Ask the child which of the following would hold more than one liter: a juice box, a bathtub, a bucket, an aquarium, and a glass. Use various tools from the kitchen to verify and check answers. Try other measurement units, such as gallon, pint, or quart. If possible, prepare simple recipes together that give the child the opportunity to review and practice measurements.

Temperature

Place a thermometer outside and have the child record the readings for a week. Use an almanac to find the average minimum and maximum temperature for two months in two different cities, including your own. How does this information compare with the student's findings? Ask the child to describe or illustrate the appropriate clothes to wear in each city for the two months. Given the temperatures, what outdoor activities would be appropriate? Record ideas or drawings in a weather journal.

Time

Until now, the child has probably practiced telling time from the hour to the quarter hour. In third grade, children begin to tell time to the minute. Help the child discover that the right half of the clock represents minutes after the hour and the left half of the clock is minutes before or to. Review the concept of skip counting to point out that it is easier to count the minutes when telling time by fives than it is by ones.

Children also begin to consider elapsed time. For success with this skill, it is critical that children count on from the starting time to the ending time to accurately determine how much time has elapsed. To practice, look through cookbooks to find the number of minutes needed to prepare various dishes. To have the meal ready for dinner, when should the cook start preparing the dish?

Ask the child to keep an activities journal in which he or she records the beginning and ending times for various activities during the day, such as walking the dog, taking a bath, or playing a game. Use subtraction to determine how much time each took. Extend this activity by having the child keep track of family activities over a weekend.

Select two distant locations and read the bus and plane schedules (available at a travel agency) to determine how long it will take to travel between two cities. Which method is the quickest way to travel? Which method is the cheapest way to travel?

Help the child make a calendar and post it in a prominent place. Pose questions to help him or her use the information. How many more days until the next holiday? How many Mondays are there this month? What is the date for the third Thursday? Help the student create a calendar for his or her notebook to use to record assignments and plan for long term projects.

Conversions

As you work with the child in developing measuring skills, keep in mind that not too much time should be spent converting a measurement from standard to metric. It is more beneficial for the child to develop some sense of the sizes of the units he or she uses to measure. A centimeter is about the width of a little finger. A liter is a bit more than a quart. A meter is a little more than a yard. Encourage the child to find useful approximations to develop his or her ability to predict the appropriate measurement unit to use for a specific task.

Marvelous Measurement

Circle the correct U.S. customary unit for measuring each item.

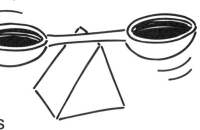

1 water in a bathtub   gallons   inches

2 soup in a bowl   liters   cups

3 a sack of potatoes   cups   pounds

4 the distance to the moon   miles   centimeters

Find the perimeter of the figure.

5

9 cm

3 cm   3 cm

9 cm

_____ cm

Find the area of the figure.

6

_____ units square

Write the correct time under each clock.

7

_____

8

_____

9

_____

Look at each clock. Tell what time it will be . . .

in 2 hours

| 6:25 |

10

_____

in 30 minutes

| 1:20 |

11

_____

in 20 minutes

| 3:45 |

12

_____

 **Name**

What's the Measurement?

Measure the length to the nearest centimeter.

_____   _____

1 _____ cm   **2** _____ cm

Circle the better unit of measure for each.

3	the distance between 2 cities	feet	miles
4	the width of a room	meters	kilometers
5	the time it takes to brush your teeth	hours	minutes
6	water in a fish bowl	liters	milliliters
7	milk in a cereal bowl	gallons	cups
8	the distance across a lake	inches	miles
9	the width of a television screen	inches	yards
10	the length of your foot	meters	centimeters

Find the perimeter.   **Find the area.**

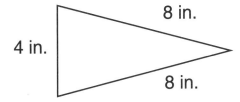

4 in.   8 in.   8 in.

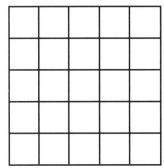

11 _____ in.   **12** _____ square units

FS122131 The Tutor's Handbook: Math Grade 3

 Name

Measuring Time and Temperature 1

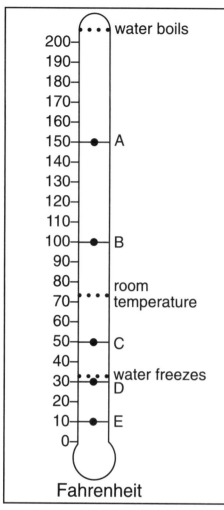

water boils
200
190
180
170
160
150 — A
140
130
120
110
100 — B
90
80
70 — room temperature
60
50 — C
40
30 — water freezes
D
20
10 — E
0

Fahrenheit

Give the temperature for each mark on the thermometer.

1 A _____ F

2 B _____ F

3 C _____ F

4 D _____ F

5 E _____ F

Circle the best temperature for each.

6 a glass of ice water   40° F   150° F

7 going ice skating   70° F   30° F

8 a very hot day   100° F   65° F

9 Which temperature would feel comfortable?   70° F   110° F

Write the correct time.

10 _____   **11** _____   **12** _____

FS122131 The Tutor's Handbook: Math Grade 3

 Name

Measuring Time and Temperature 2

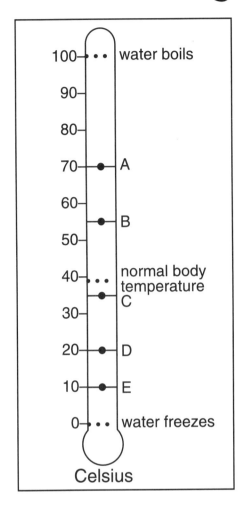

Give the temperature for each mark on the thermometer.

1 A _____ C

2 B _____ C

3 C _____ C

4 D _____ C

5 E _____ C

Circle the best temperature for each.

6 a tub of hot bath water   50° C   90° C

7 a very hot summer day   10° C   40° C

8 a cup of hot chocolate   20° C   80° C

Write the correct time.

9 _____

10 _____

11 _____

What time will it be in 4 hours?

3:28

in 40 minutes?

5:45

in 15 minutes?

8:27

12 _____

13 _____

14 _____

FS122131 The Tutor's Handbook: Math Grade 3

Measurement Mania

Circle the best metric unit for measuring each item.

1. juice in a glass   gallons   liters

2. the weight of a baby   kilograms   inches

3. a box of cereal   meters   grams

4. the area of a yard   kilometers   feet

Find the perimeter of the figure.   **Find the area of the figure.**

5.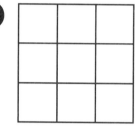
   5 in.
   5 in.   5 in.
   5 in.

6.

_____ in.   _____ square units

Write the correct time under each clock.

7.    8.    9.

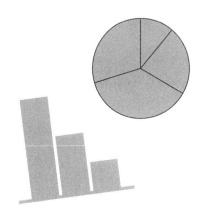

CONCEPTS THIRD GRADERS SHOULD KNOW

- collect, organize, graph, and interpret data
- line graphs, bar graphs, pictographs, and tables
- tally marks
- probability (likelihood) of an event

Pictograph

In a pictograph a picture or symbol is used to stand for one or more objects. To accurately interpret the data, children need to recognize that the key on a pictograph tells them how many of the objects each symbol represents. They should also be able to explain how to interpret a half symbol on a pictograph. Help the student locate this information on various pictographs you have collected.

Line Graph

A line graph uses line segments to connect the points on a graph. This tool is used to show how data changes over time. Working with line graphs also familiarizes children with ordered pairs, where the first number represents the horizontal axis and the second number in the pair represents the vertical axis. Observe and record the weather conditions for a week. Compare information you record to that given on a television newscast, in a newspaper, or on the internet. Have the child use the data to create a line graph and discuss the results.

Bar Graph

Third graders examine and interpret bar graphs, as well. On this type of graph, children may need to interpret a halfway point. To avoid errors in interpretation, suggest that the student use a straight edge as a guide when reading bar graphs. Choose five food packages from the kitchen. Look at the nutritional information listed on the packages to determine the number of fat grams in one serving. Help the child record and interpret this information on a bar graph.

Tally Chart

A tally chart is another way that third graders learn to record, organize, and compare information collected. Children in third grade are often asked to use the data collected in a tally chart to create either a pictograph or a bar graph. Help the child recognize that it is easier to count groups of five than it is to count tally marks one at a time. Teach the student to make a cross hatch for the fifth tally to facilitate counting the information.

Helpful Hint: Vary the orientation of graphs. Students need to learn to interpret both horizontal and vertical graphs.

Conduct a Survey

Reinforce the skills learned in previous tutoring sessions by asking the student to pose a question to a variety of people and record the informa- tion. When the child chooses the ques-

> **Helpful Hint:** Taking a survey helps students develop communication skills as they collect the desired information.

tion, he or she has ownership and is more moti- vated to elicit responses. What is your favorite tele- vision show? What do you like best for dinner? It might be helpful to assist the child in creating a table on which to record the results—one column for the responses and another column to tally responses. You might suggest three or four possi- ble responses for the people to respond to. This will help the child organize better.

Once the information has been collected, ask the child to represent it in a graph. Encourage the student to examine the data. Are there any pat- terns in the numbers represented? Help the child to represent the information using the fewest number of symbols for each item. If all of the num- bers are even, suggest using an even number in the key. If all of the data ends in a 5 or a 0, count- ing by fives would make more sense.

Once the graph is complete, help the child ana- lyze the results. Pose questions that require the child to make comparisons or predictions. If you asked 10 more people the same question, what would be the most likely response?

Probability

Probability is the prediction or analysis of the likelihood that a certain event will occur. It is expressed as the ratio of the number of favorable outcomes (numerator) to the number of total pos- sible outcomes (denominator). Something is equally likely to happen if all of the possible out- comes have the same chance of occurring. If a spinner is equally divided and has each color or number on it only once, there is an equally likely chance of spinning each color or number. If one color occurs more than the others, the chances are not equally likely.

Have the student create equally likely and not equally likely spinners using heavy cardboard. The pointer can be made from a heavy card and attached to the spinner with a brass brad. Practice spinning both types of spinners and record the results. Graph and discuss the results. How likely is it to spin a particular color? Which color did you spin the most? How is the probability different on each spinner? Vary this activity by using coins or rolling dice.

 Name

Recycling Drive

A third grade class collected the following items for recycling. Make a pictograph to organize the information. Answer the questions.

Containers Collected	
aluminum	65
large plastic	40
small plastic	70
large glass	55
small glass	20
cardboard boxes	45

Containers Collected	
aluminum	
large plastic	
small plastic	
large glass	
small glass	
cardboard boxes	

key: ☐ = 10 containers

Did the class collect

1 more plastic or glass containers? _____

2 more large or small containers? _____

Look at the spinner. Answer the questions.

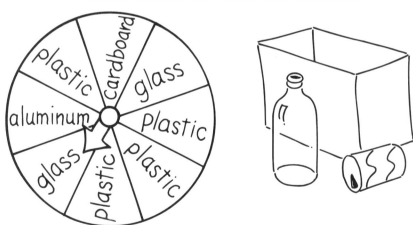

3 What is the probability of landing on plastic? _____

4 What is the probability of landing on glass? _____

FS122131 The Tutor's Handbook: Math Grade 3

 Name

Sports Briefing

Complete the bar graph to show the sports third graders play during recess.

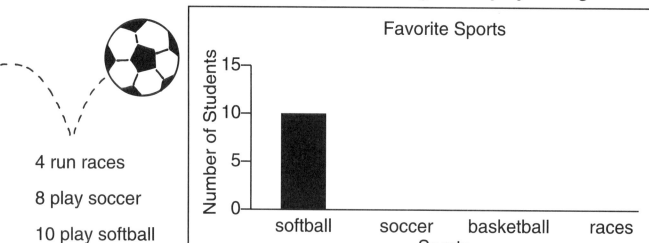

4 run races

8 play soccer

10 play softball

14 play basketball

Answer these questions using the bar graph.

1 How many more students play basketball than soccer? _____

2 How many students play a sport that uses a ball? _____

3 How many more students play softball than run races? _____

4 How many students are in the third grade? _____

Look at the spinner. Answer the questions.

5 What is the probability you would spin an even number? _____

6 What is the probability you would spin a 6? _____

7 What is the probability you would spin an odd number? _____

 Name

Snack Attack

What is your favorite snack?

Mary–popcorn	John–candy	David–chips	Daniel–pretzels
Tom–candy	Keisha–crackers	Alicia–candy	Tammy–candy
Asia–popcorn	Sam–chips	Jon–popcorn	Quan–fruit
Tiffany–chips	Lisa–pretzels	Anna–crackers	Mark–fruit
Rand–popcorn	Jack–popcorn	Lois–popcorn	Diane–candy
Catrina–chips	Karen–candy	Bill–candy	Carol–pretzels
Devon–crackers	Kathy–chips	Matthew–popcorn	Lynn–popcorn
Jorge–fruit	Ken–crackers	Pedro–candy	Stacy–candy

Organize the results of the survey in a tally chart.

1

	Favorite snacks
popcorn	
candy	
pretzels	
fruit	
chips	
crackers	

Use your tally chart to help you answer these questions.

2 Which two snacks got the same number of votes?

_____ and _____

3 How many children like a salty snack? _____

On the back of this paper, make a bar graph to show the results of the survey.

FS122131 The Tutor's Handbook: Math Grade 3

Wacky Weather

Complete the bar graph to show the weather during the month of March.

Tally Chart	
卌	sunny days
||| 卌	cloudy days
|| 卌 卌	windy days
	卌	rainy days

Weather in March

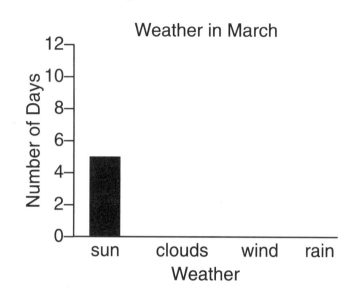

Use the information on the graph to help you answer these questions.

1 How many more windy days than rainy days? _____

2 How many sunny days? _____

3 How many days would you need an umbrella? _____

Look at the spinner.
Answer the questions.

4 What is the weather condition you would be least likely to spin? _____

5 What is the weather condition you would most likely spin? _____

FS122131 The Tutor's Handbook: Math Grade 3

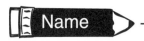

Name ____

Book Survey

The tally chart shows third graders' favorite types of books. Make a bar graph to organize the data. Make two statements about the information on the graph.

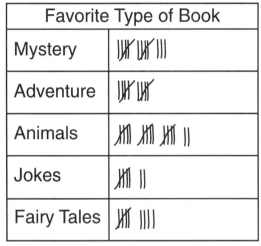

Favorite Type of Book	
Mystery	||||/ ||||/ |||
Adventure	||||/ ||||/
Animals	||||/ ||||/ ||||/ ||
Jokes	||||/ ||
Fairy Tales	||||/ ||||

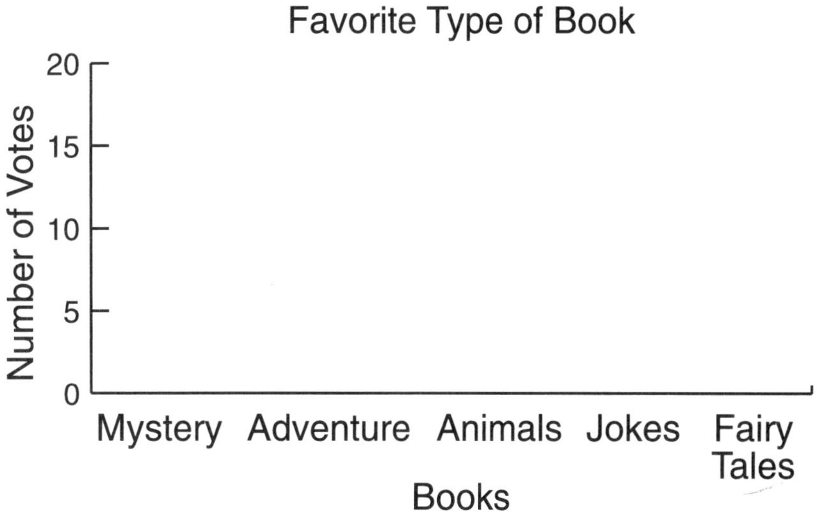

Favorite Type of Book
Number of Votes
20
15
10
5
0
Mystery
Adventure
Animals
Jokes
Fairy Tales
Books

1. ____.
2. ____.

Pretend that the following coins are placed in a bag. Imagine that you are asked to reach in the bag and pull out one coin at a time, without looking. Answer the questions.

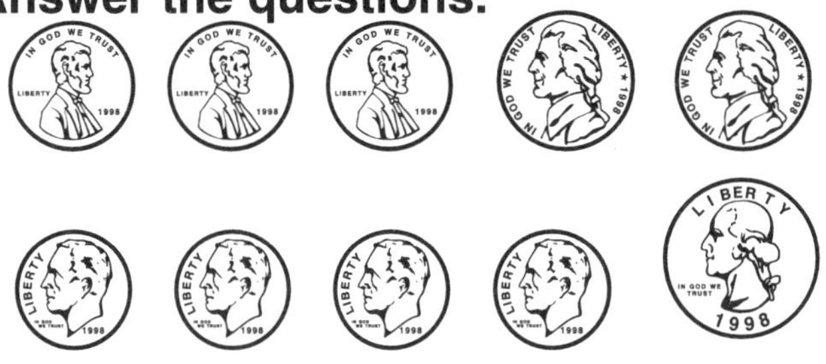

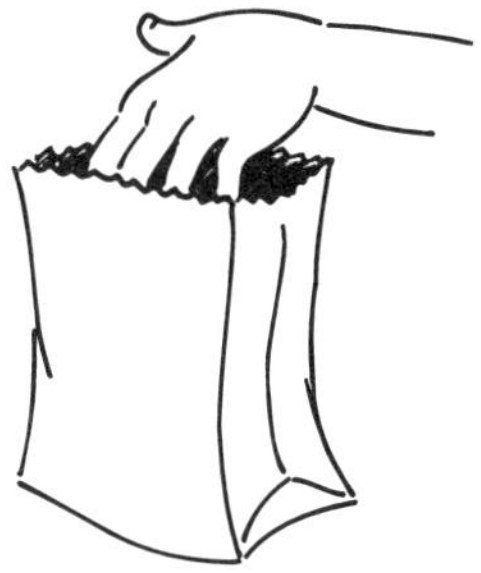

What are the chances of pulling out

3. a nickel? ____________ chances out of ________________.
4. a dime? ______________ chances out of _________________.
5. a quarter? ___________ chances out of ________________.

It is important to help the child understand that he or she is developing a variety of strategies that will help him or her solve math problems. A strategy is simply a plan that may be used to solve a problem. Choosing an appropriate strategy is the challenge. A sufficient understanding of the different strategies the child has mastered will enable him or her to think the problem through and select the best one to use to solve a particular problem.

Helpful Hint: Be sensitive to the child's reading level. Let the child do the math, but help him or her with the reading.

If the child is unsuccessful in solving a problem, help him or her with an alternative approach to the problem. Talking through a number of different problems helps the child develop more sophisticated problem-solving skills. In fact, the process that the student goes through to solve the problem is as important as the correct solution.

As you help the student solve a variety of problems, encourage him or her to recall some of the strategies he or she has developed.

Can you make a table or graph with the information?

Would it help you to draw a picture?

Can you combine some of the numbers to make them easier to work with?

What is the problem asking?

Which operation should you use?

What are the key words in the problem that help you know what to do?

Does the problem require more than one step? Which step is first?

Is there information missing that is needed to solve the problem?

Does the problem contain unnecessary information?

Can you find a pattern?

Can you make a guess and test the answer?

As you work with the child, remember the benefit of having him or her talk about his or her thinking process. Respond and ask additional questions that will help the child discover that there is often more than one way to solve a given problem. Help the child evaluate these possibilities and determine the best course of action.

Remind children of the steps necessary to solve a problem.

think	What is the problem asking?
search	What facts does the problem give? How will I solve it?
solve	Compute the answer—this may require more than one step.
check	Does my answer make sense? Does it answer the question?

Consider listing these steps on a chart and continually review them until they become automatic.

People Problems

Solve each problem. In each box, show the strategy you used.

---

1 Tommy jogs every morning before school. Last week, he ran 4 miles on Monday, 2 miles on Tuesday, 3 on Wednesday, 5 on Thursday, and 1 on Friday. How far did Tommy jog last week?

2 Adam carries 2 pounds of newspapers each time he goes to the recycling bin. How many trips will he make to carry 12 pounds?

---

3 Amanda buys 2 alarm clocks that cost $9.42 each. How much money did Amanda spend?

4 Amy and Martha read 48 books altogether during the summer. Amy read 6 books more than Martha. How many books did Amy read?

FS122131 The Tutor's Handbook: Math Grade 3

 **Name**

What's Missing?

Read each problem. What do you need to know before you can solve the problem? Tell what information is missing.

1 Mrs. Jones wants to serve ice-cream cake at 7:00 p.m. When should she take the cake out of the freezer?

_____

2 Eugene has 3 rolls of film to take pictures on his family vacation. How many pictures can he take?

_____

3 Three classes collected can goods for the food drive. Room 19 collected 43 cans. Room 23 brought in 57 cans. How many cans did all three classes collect?

_____

4 Mr. Ramirez has 32 children in his class. There are 18 girls and 14 boys. Seven children were absent on Wednesday. How many girls were in class on Wednesday?

_____

5 The vacuum cleaner at the car wash costs 75¢ for 10 minutes. Laura went to the car wash at 11:00 a.m. How much did she spend to use the vacuum?

_____

6 Four parents baked 3 dozen cupcakes for the school bake sale. How much money will the school make if they sell all of the cupcakes?

_____

 **Name**

The Picnic Problem

Circle which operation you would use to solve each problem. Then solve each problem.

1	There are 4 picnic tables. Six people can sit at each table. How many people can sit at tables at the picnic?	addition subtraction multiplication division
2	The students brought 4 cherry pies and 10 apple pies to the picnic. How many pies did they bring in all?	addition subtraction multiplication division
3	The children played games at the picnic. Twelve children played soccer and 18 played baseball. How many more children played baseball than soccer?	addition subtraction multiplication division
4	How many children were on each team for the baseball and soccer games?	addition subtraction multiplication division

FS122131 The Tutor's Handbook: Math Grade 3

 Name

Write Your Own

Student	Number of Crayons
Lynn	5
George	8
Samantha	12
Deangelo	64
Maria	16
Shelly	24
Tran	13

Use the information given in the chart.

1 Write a subtraction story problem.
Solve.

_____

_____

_____

_____

_____

Answer: _____

2 Write a multiplication story problem.
Solve.

_____

_____

_____

_____

_____

Answer: _____

Name

Proud Problem Solver

Solve each problem. In each box, show the strategy you used to solve the problem.

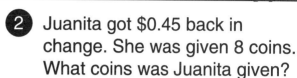

---

1 Last February, 16 inches of snow fell in Boulder, Colorado. This was 8 inches less than the record. What is the record?

2 Juanita got $0.45 back in change. She was given 8 coins. What coins was Juanita given?

---

3 Louise can plant 5 bean seeds in 8 minutes. How long will it take her to plant 40 beans?

4 You are buying a book that costs $3.25. You give the cashier a five dollar bill. How much change should you get back?

 Name

Let's Review

Answer each question.

1 What is the number for 6 thousands, 4 hundreds, 8 tens, 9 ones?

_____

2 What is the value of the 7 in 5,726? _____

Round each number.

3 Round to the nearest hundred. 742 _____

4 Round to the nearest ten. 4,587 _____

Add or subtract.

5
```
   79
 + 83
```

6
```
 $40.27
- 17.64
```

7
```
   3,211
 + 1,824
```

8
```
   608
    72
 + 394
```

9 Write the four number sentences for the fact family 5, 8, 13.

_____   _____

_____   _____

10 Write the numbers in order from smallest to greatest.

6,812   6,309   4,579   4,532

FS122131 The Tutor's Handbook: Math Grade 3

 Name

Let's Review

Multiply or divide.

1   7
   x 4

2   2
   x 9

3   5
   x 8

4   6
   x 3

5 6 x 6 = _____

6 4 x 8= _____

7 5 x 7 = _____

8 48 ÷ 6 = _____

9 35 ÷ 7 = _____

10 81 ÷ 9 = _____

11 $2\overline{)12}$

12 $5\overline{)40}$

13 $8\overline{)32}$

14 $3\overline{)12}$

15 Give four number sentences for the fact family 6, 9, 54.

_____   _____

_____   _____

Complete each number pattern.

16 515, _____, 535, _____, 555, _____, 575

17 82, _____, _____, 88, _____, 92

FS122131 The Tutor's Handbook: Math Grade 3

 **Name**

Let's Review

Use an inch ruler to measure.

1 _____ inches   _____

Circle the best measurement.

2 What is the best measure for a jug of apple cider?

gallons   cups

3 What is the best measure for the length of a pencil?

centimeters   meters

4 Find the perimeter.

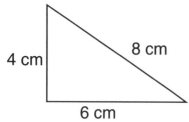

4 cm   8 cm

6 cm

5 Find the area.

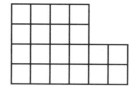

_____   _____

6 Write the time showing on the clock.

7 What time will it be in one hour?

6:48

_____   _____

FS122131 The Tutor's Handbook: Math Grade 3

 Name _____

Geometry

Let's Review

Write the name for each figure.

1

2

_____   _____

Look at the shape and tell how many of each.

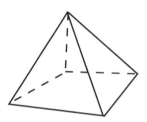

3 _____ faces

4 _____ edges

5 _____ corners

Write *yes* or *no*.

Are the two shapes congruent?

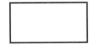

Does the dashed line show a line of symmetry?

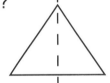

6 _____

7 _____

8 Plot the coordinates on the grid.

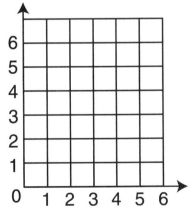

(1,1) (1, 6) (5,1)

Connect the points.
What shape is made?

_____

FS122131 The Tutor's Handbook: Math Grade 3

Let's Review

For every three sandwiches, six ounces of meat and three ounces of cheese are used. Complete the chart and answer the questions that follow.

sandwiches	1	2	3	4	5	6
meat	2		6			
cheese	1		3			

1 How much cheese is used on one sandwich? _____ ounce

2 How much meat is used on one sandwich? _____ ounces

3 How much meat is used on five sandwiches _____ ounces

4 How much cheese is used on two sandwiches? _____ ounces

Solve the problem. Show the strategy you used to solve the problem.

5 Thomas has 2 brothers. The sum of their ages is 12. The difference between their ages is 4 years. How old is each brother?

_____ and _____

Literature to Read Together

Use these suggested books to help the student develop math skills.

Alexander, Who Used to Be Rich Last Sunday by Judith Viorst (Atheneum, 1985).
A boy spends his only dollar on a variety of irresistible objects.

Anno's Hat Tricks by Mitsumasa Anno and Akihiro Nozaki (Philomel, 1985).
Three children use logic to guess the color of the hats on their heads.

Anno's Mysterious Multiplying Jar by Masaichiro Anno and Mitsumasa Anno (Philomel, 1983).
This book introduces the concept of factors through simple text and engaging pictures.

Counting on Frank by Rod Clement (Gareth Stevens, 1991).
A measuring maniac boy causes the reader to take a new look at ordinary objects.

Each Orange Had 8 Slices: A Counting Book by Paul Giganti (Morrow, William and Co., 1992).
This book introduces counting and simple addition.

The Go-Around Dollar by Barbara Johnston Adams (Four Winds Press, 1992).
This fun book explains how money changes hands and includes unusual facts about money.

The Greedy Triangle by Marilyn Burns (Scholastic, 1995).
A bored triangle goes to see the shapeshifter and becomes a quadrilateral. This book is an excellent introduction to polygons and shapes.

How Big Is a Foot? by Rolf Myller (Atheneum, 1969).
The king orders a new bed to be built, but the lack of a standard measurement in the kingdom makes the results amusing.

Images 3: The Ultimate Coloring Experience by Roger Burrows (Running Press, 1994).
Children create unique art as they discover a variety of patterns.

Inch By Inch by Leo Lionni (Astor-Honor, 1962).
An inchworm proudly measures a variety of birds and other objects.

The King's Chessboard by David Birch (Dial, 1988).
A wise man outsmarts a king when he chooses a reward of one grain of rice to be doubled each day for 64 days.

The Line Up Book by Marisabina Russo (Greenwillow, 1986).
A boy uses all of his toys to make one line to the kitchen when his mother calls him for lunch.

Math Curse by Jon Scieszka and Lane Smith (Viking, 1995).
This book tells the humorous story of a girl who wakes up one morning and has to use math for everything she does.

The Night of the Moonjellies by Mark Shasha (Simon and Schuster, 1992).
A boy and his grandmother return a moonjelly to the sea and explore money, addition, and problem solving.

Opt: An Illusionary Tale by Arline and Joseph Baum (Puffin, 1987).
A royal family shows a variety of optical illusions and measurement in an engaging manner.

The 12 Circus Rings by Seymour Chwast (Harcourt Brace, 1993).
This book uses the structure of the familiar "Twelve Days of Christmas" to engage children in a variety of number explorations.

263 Brain Busters: Just How Smart Are You, Anyway? by Louis Phillips (Penguin, 1985).
This wonderful book tests math, logic, and listening skills in a clever manner.

The Village of Round and Square Houses by Ann Grifalconi (Little, Brown and Company, 1986).
An African grandmother tells the story of a volcanic eruption which led to the village men living in square houses and the women in round houses.

What Comes in 2s, 3s, and 4s? by Suzanne Aker (Simon and Schuster, 1990).
This book uses common objects to help children see multiplication in everyday life.

Answers

Page 16
1. 4,000 + 600 + 80 + 2
2. 700 + 90 +6
3. 6,082
4. 3,469
5. 621, 372, 298
6. 592, 571, 538
7. 430
8. 380
9. 800
10. 3,700
11. $0.62
12. 109
13. $7.51
14. 597
15. 35
16. $3.84
17. 4,711

Page 17
1. 243
2. 228
3. 102
4. $3.65
5. 171
6. 54
7. 104, 75
   179
   100, 79
8. 60, 109
   169
   89, 80
9. 1,300, 1,310
10. 8,700, 8,680
11. 300
12. 3,000

Page 18
1. 34
2. 141
3. 423
4. $1.29
5. 1,325
6. 536
7. 329, 197, 546
8. 700, 805, 199
9. 3,867, 3,212, 3,107
10. 587, 403, 215
11. 3,113

Page 19
1. 588
2. 5,000
3. $10.25
4. 2,709
5. 6,009
6. 548
7. 418, 1005
   1423
   598, 825
8. 575, 450
   125
   304, 179
9. 800
10. 6,000
11. 80

Page 20
1. 8,000 + 200 + 70 + 4
2. 400 + 70 + 8
3. 4,627
4. 242
5. 2,472, 3,612, 3,678
6. 730
7. 690
8. 1,900
9. 500
10. $ .79
11. 1,453
12. 376
13. 1,485
14. $4.11

Page 24
1. 30, 33, 35
2. 45, 48, 51
3. 4, 8, 12, 16, 20
4. 18, 21, 15, 6, 12, 0, 3
   (counterclockwise)
5. 35, 0, 10, 40, 20, 5, 15
   (counterclockwise)
6. 7 + 8 = 15
   8 + 7 = 15
   15 − 7 = 8
   15 − 8 = 8
7. 21 ÷ 3 = 7
   21 ÷ 7 = 3
   7 x 3 = 21
   3 x 7 = 21
8. 4 x 8 = 32
   8 x 4 = 32
   32 ÷ 4 = 8
   32 ÷ 8 = 4

Page 25
1. 6
2. 24
3. 12
4. 45
5. 16
6. 9
7. 9
8. 8
9. 8
10. 12, 3, 9, 18, 24
11. 0, 10, 12, 14, 16
12. 2, 5, 8, 7, 3
13. 40, 8, 24, 6, 12, 4

Page 26
1. 42
2. 49
3. 36
4. 32
5. 63
6. 5
7. 7
8. 6
9. 5
10. 49, 42, 56, 35
11. 8, 7, 9, 3
12. 8 x 6 = 48
    48 ÷ 8 = 6
    48 ÷ 6 = 8
13. 56 ÷ 7 = 8
    7 x 8 = 56
    8 x 7 = 56
14. 42 ÷ 6 = 7
    6 x 7 = 42
    7 x 6 = 42

Page 27
1. 565, 665, 765
2. 22, 29, 36
3. 6, 9, 12, 15, 18
4. 0, 49, 35, 14, 42, 28,
   21 (counterclockwise)
5. 18, 9, 27, 45, 63, 36,
   54 (counterclockwise)
6. 9 + 7 = 16
   7 + 9 = 16
   16 − 9 = 7
   16 − 7 = 9
7. 7 x 4 = 28
   4 x 7 = 28
   28 ÷ 4 = 7
   28 ÷ 7 = 4

Page 30
1. sphere 0, 0, 0, 1
   cube 8, 12, 6, 0
2. yes
3. yes
4. rectangle

Page 31
1. greater
2. right
3. less
4. greater
5. 5
6. 4
7. 5
8. Answers will vary
9.

10. Answers will vary

Page 32
1. yes
2. no
3. yes
4. flip
5. turn
6. slide
7. triangle

Page 33
1. cube
2. cylinder
3. pyramid
4. sphere
5. rectangular prism
6. cylinder
7. cube
8. cone
9. Answers will vary
10. Answers will vary
11. Answers will vary

Page 34
1. triangle
2. cone
3. cylinder
4. yes
5.
6. right
7. less

Answers

Page 38
1. gallons
2. cups
3. pounds
4. miles
5. 24 cm
6. 16 square units
7. 1:20
8. 11:40
9. 3:25
10. 8:25
11. 1:50
12. 4:05

Page 39
1. 8 cm
2. 3 cm
3. miles
4. meters
5. minutes
6. liters
7. cups
8. miles
9. inches
10. centimeters
11. 20 in.
12. 25 square units

Page 40
1. 150°
2. 100°
3. 50°
4. 30°
5. 10°
6. 40°
7. 30°
8. 100°
9. 70°
10. 8:14
11. 4:28
12. 3:48

Page 41
1. 70°
2. 55°
3. 35°
4. 20°
5. 10°
6. 50°
7. 40°
8. 80°
9. 3:12
10. 11:48
11. 7:33
12. 7:28
13. 6:25
14. 8:42

Page 42
1. liters
2. kilograms
3. grams
4. feet
5. 20 in.
6. 9 square units
7. 4:25
8. 11:40
9. 1:50

Page 45
1. plastic
2. large
3. $\frac{4}{8}$
4. $\frac{2}{8}$

Page 46
1. 6
2. 32
3. 6
4. 36
5. $\frac{4}{8}$
6. $\frac{1}{8}$
7. $\frac{4}{8}$

Page 47
1. popcorn 8
   candy 9
   pretzels 3
   fruit 3
   chips 5
   crackers 4
2. pretzels and fruit
3. 20

Page 48
1. 6
2. 5
3. 6
4. rain
5. sun

Page 49
1. Answers will vary
2. Answers will vary
3. 2, 10
4. 4, 10
5. 1, 10

Page 51
1. 15 miles
2. 6 trips
3. $18.84
4. 27

Page 52
1. how long the cake needs to thaw
2. how many pictures on a roll
3. how many cans collected by third class
4. how many girls were absent on Wed.
5. how long she vacuumed
6. how much each cupcake cost

Page 53
1. multiplication, 24 people
2. addition, 14 pies
3. subtraction, 6 more
4. division, soccer—6, baseball—9

Page 54
Answers will vary

Page 55
1. 24
2. 1 quarter, 1 dime, 1 nickel, 5 pennies
3. 64 minutes
4. $1.75

Page 56
1. 6,489
2. 700
3. 700
4. 4,590
5. 162
6. $22.63
7. 5,035
8. 1,074
9. 8 + 5 = 13
   5 + 8 = 13
   13 − 8 = 5
   13 − 5 = 8
10. 4,532, 4,579, 6,309, 6,812

Page 57
1. 28
2. 18
3. 40
4. 18
5. 36
6. 32
7. 35
8. 8
9. 5
10. 9
11. 6
12. 8
13. 4
14. 4
15. 6 x 9 = 54
    9 x 6 = 54
    54 ÷ 6 = 9
    54 ÷ 9 = 6
16. 525, 545, 565
17. 84, 86, 90

Page 58
1. 3 in.
2. gallons
3. centimeters
4. 18 cm
5. 20 sq. units
6. 1:24
7. 7:48

Page 59
1. cylinder
2. rectangular prism
3. 5
4. 8
5. 5
6. yes
7. yes
8. triangle

Page 60

sandwiches	1	2	3	4	5	6
meat	2	4	6	8	10	12
cheese	1	2	3	4	5	6

1. 1 oz.
2. 2 oz.
3. 10 oz.
4. 2 oz.
5. 8 and 4

FS122131 The Tutor's Handbook: Math Grade 3